This Book Belongs To:

....

Up & Down New York

Up & Down New York

by Tony Sarg

Preface by
Jonathan Adler

UNIVERSE

Contents

Preface

I love New York. The stinky bits, the gorgeous bits, the weirdos, the hairdos—it's fabulous. I don't care if I get drenched by a passing bus or spat at by a homeless person on my way to work. The freaky occurrences and improbable people are what make this town tick.

But, if one bleak day, the unthinkable happens and I cease to be enthralled by my adopted hometown, I'm going to pull out Tony Sarg's New York to remind me of the spirit of La Grande Pomme. It's all there—the traffic, the society dames, the Wall Street dudes, the fops, the rich, the poor, the fat, the thin, the black, the white, the immigrants, the outdoor markets—so vivid one can almost smell the streets.

In Tony Sarg's paws, the mayhem of New York becomes magic. The smells are the smells from flower stands, the noise is the sound of commerce, the daily contretemps are fodder for great anecdotes, and so what if you can't get a taxi—who wants a taxi anyway when there's so much more fun to be had walking? These pictures make you feel like New York's legendary rents are worth it to join in the fun!

That this book is from 1927 is startling—contemporary New York is instantly recognizable on its pages. The Village is The Village, the subway is the subway, Chinatown is Chinatown, and the same people have come here to pursue their dreams. And Le Sarg treats them all with a mix of love and humor.

Today's artists have a lot to learn from Sarg. Like a Hokusai print, these pictures are flawlessly composed. The colors dance around the frame and the lines zig and zag like like a modern jazz arrangement. Sarg sucks you in with his formal mastery and then lets the fun of the city unfold.

Thank God this love letter to New York is being reprinted. Now, if anybody ever impugns my town, I can just open Tony Sarg's New York and show them the majesty.

Jonathan Adler

Introduction

When I was living in England I painted a series of pictures which was published under the title "Humours of London." They were all birdseye views, such as one sees looking down into a busy street from a window of a sky-scraper. These birdseye views—or panorama views, as some of my friends call them—depended for their interest, not upon the locality chosen, but upon the humor of the figures which were introduced into the pictures.

These figures were depicted in such action as the locality inspired. For instance, in a drawing of the Royal Academy, a fashionable crowd was pictured at an exhibition and the interest of the drawing lay, not in a reproduction of the Academy itself, but in the people looking at the pictures. One saw the painter admiring his own canvas, the bored businessman, who had been unwillingly dragged to the exhibition by his women-folk, and many other figures expressing those "touches of nature" which appeal to the humorous-minded spectator.

In the like manner another drawing showed a bank holiday at Hampstead Heath with crowds of simple people making merry in a kind of English Coney Island fashion.

No subject was chosen simply because it was a charming scene, or a superb piece of architecture, but always because it was a centre of activity—a meeting-place, where numbers of human beings might be observed in action.

This new series of drawings treats New York in the same manner as the earlier series (of which they are the logical outcome) treated London.

All of the pictures are birdseye views and are executed in a manner which invites investigation. I have chosen this device, because it gives opportunity for the use of a great many figures. When the artist draws his picture on the level, the figures in the foreground obliterate those in the background; but, observed from above the figures do not hide each other. Hence, the birdseye view.

Besides, this treatment presents many interesting problems in foreshortening; and sometimes requires the solving of difficult questions of locale—how much of a building or a scene to introduce in order to suggest the background which is the source of action for the figures. For instance, in a railroad station, the action and humor of the figures grows out of the functions of the station. In drawing the Grand Central Station in New York

I have presented a complete interior view. The characteristic gestures of people buying tickets, digging up change, carrying luggage, running for trains, getting their pockets picked—these gestures have elements of humor and they are directly related to the locality which is pictured.

The moment of action is the moment of humor, which the artist seizes upon. Two men talking passively at a street-corner express little enough, but let them fall into a heated argument with gestures—and there is a subject one positively itches to draw.

"Every little movement has a meaning of its own" might be the slogan of the humorous artist.

New York abounds in types and centers, which provide an endless fund of material and suggestion. There is no street-corner where the amenities of the road are forgotten. There is comedy stuff in the policeman who calls down a faulty chauffeur, but blossoms into a wide grin when he discovers that the said chauffeur is Irish! There is humor in the clothes-and-suit pushcart-man on Sixth Avenue, who trundles his little wagon in and out among the taxicabs to the accompaniment of much cursing and some priceless repartee; in the stretching of necks to see what the Extra is about, without buying the paper; and in the half-hearted tip of a hat, meant as a cautious advance to a lady.

We are all funny and never more so than when we are unconscious of it—the aristocrat no less than the laborer, although the gestures of the former must be more subtly delineated then those of the latter, who is more generous in his expression.

Nor is this quality confined to the human family. The humors of the animal world are infinite. Two dogs nosing each other in the street are often comical; and how delicious is the truckman's fox-terrier, sassing back at the policeman, who has just called his master down: All the man wants to say is written on his face—and what the dog, in happy canine freedom, is saying, is a plenty. Even the policeman has to laugh.

Wet and windy days, with blown hats and skirts, and umbrellas turned inside-out—plus the indignation which these mischances arouse in their victims—afford opportunity for funny pictures, too; and the subway is a gold mine. Sometimes I play a kind of game in the subway, studying the feet across the aisle, without looking at the faces, trying to imagine what kind of heads belong to each pair of feet. Feet are expressive, surprisingly so. They are not simply large feet or small, beautiful or ugly;

they express a variety of things; there are old feet and young, funny feet, vain feet, feet in bad taste, pathetic feet.

Crowding around the animal-cages at the Bronx Zoo, catching and missing trains at the railroad stations, reading and lounging at the Public Library, dodging automobiles around Dead Man's Corner, bargaining over the push-carts in the Ghetto, jostling each other on the Great White Way, are always people, a never-ending procession of people of all kinds, from every walk of life—people who are the actors in an infinity of small comedies.

It is so that I see New York and so that I wish to picture it—a city depicted in terms of people.

Tony Sarg

Grand Central Station

A feverish moment in the big depot.

Public Library

The literary center of the metropolis.

Museum of Natural History

Another skirmish in the evolution war.

The Aquarium

Open season at the big pond in our town.

Sixth Avenue "L" at Thirty-third Street

A restful moment in Greeley Square, where Broadway meets Sixth Avenue.

Peacock Alley in the Waldorf Astoria

Struts and other poses in the Waldorf lobby.

Times Square

One crossroad in our town—where Broadway meets Seventh Avenue.

Twenty-third Street Ferry Slip

Our town offers yachting to its thousands of commuters.

Metropolitan Museum of Art

Exhibits, human and otherwise, in the Hall of Casts.

The Ghetto

The shopping hour on the busy East Side—a street corner among the tenements.

The Flatiron Building

Lower Fifth Avenue in a forty-knot blow.

The Stock Exchange

A calm moment among our Bulls and Bears.

Washington Market

A busy day at our local vegetable patch.

Greenwich Village

Sheridan Square, the heart of the "Village," where Art is everything.

The City Hall

The heart and vocal chords of the municipality.

The Shuttle
in the Subway

Exploring one of the leading labyrinths of our subway system at Grand Central Station.

Manhattan Bridge

Where Canal Street becomes a skyline.

Customs Inspection

A session of the Inquisition in our town—customs inspection at Pier 54.

Chinatown

Where East meets West in lower New York—Pell Street in action.

The Great White Way

New York's wonderland by night.

Columbus Circle

Where Christopher Columbus surveys a scene of constant bustle.

Jefferson Market Police Court

An historic mill of justice grinding in our town.

"East Side, West Side, All Around the Town"

Studies from the Lower East Side, where all the world meets.

Snatched from the Melting Pot

Character sketches of various types in our town.

Published by Universe Publishing,
A Division of Rizzoli International Publications
300 Park Avenue South
New York, NY 10010
www.rizzoliusa.com

2007 2008 2009 2010 2011 / 10 9 8 7 6 5 4 3 2 1

Design by Willy Wong
Rizzoli Editor: Ellen Cohen
Editors: Barbara Cohen and Judith Stonehill

ISBN: 0-7893-1548-3
ISBN-13: 978-0-7893-1548-9
Library of Congress Catalogue Number: 2006939307

Printed in China

Up & Down New York is part of a series of New York Bound books.